C000129080

About the composition of the book :

The poems in the first part, "Black Moon," take us on a deep and introspective emotional journey. We encounter reflections on subjects such as illness, grief, sadness, loneliness, and the toxicity of emotions. It is a sincere and honest exploration of pain and the challenges we may encounter along life's path.

The second part, "Tomorrow at Dawn," is a light in the darkness, focusing on subjects such as love, the path to peace, acceptance, and resilience. It offers a glimpse into moments of happiness, hope, and healing. The poems in this section celebrate the beauty of life and the human capacity to find light in the darkest of times.

I BLACK MOON

The sun has set, the one that shone within
me when I was but an innocent soul.
Night has fallen, its essence quivers in
hearts, in the profound darkness.

TRAUMAS

In my mind resonate the cries of a lost
happiness,
The innocence of early years,
Laughter on the shores,
The opportunity that seeks only to live,
The joys of childhood and its abundance,
Representing the most beautiful youth,
Before life took its dance,
I remember, it was so long ago,
That short and intense period,
When I was just a child,
Carefreeness flew away like a migratory
bird,

For that lost childhood, forever I mourn.

When I write, I bare myself,
Usually, nothing comes out,
It's as if I become free,
When life inflicts harm upon me.

little notes
on
scraps of paper

_ writing

Between smiles and tears, I have grown,
Between fears and dramas,
I have faced life,
At the tender age of five,
Forced to play in the realm of adults,
Sometimes I miss the time before,

But childhood is a chapter that ends
without us knowing,

When the weight of life becomes too heavy
to bear,
I immerse myself in my memories,
To breathe more freely,
Lamenting the days when everything was
colorful.

I see him in my dreams,
Lying on that hospital bed,
Imprisoned by a fatal disease,
His soul on the brink of tears,
Yet he radiated without falsehood,
Believing in it so strongly,
To make his heart beat,
During those years filled with pain,
His inner strength illuminated the space,
As if the illness hadn't erased it,

I saw in his eyes,
Hope like nowhere else.

- Fatal hope

Not a day goes by,
Without me thinking of his smile,
His pride when he saw us laugh,
I held resentment towards the entire
world,
When I saw this disease,
Attacking his being,
Until it left him lifeless,
Illness is a hell,
That separates the body and the spirit,
It brought him lower than the ground,
Without granting him any respite,
Tears streamed down our faces,
We hoped the world would spare him,
We prayed for it all to be a cruel illusion,
But when illness prevails,
It throws us into a curve,
With heart-wrenching sorrow as our only
companion.

She kissed his hand,
Then led him on her path,
To poison him with her venom,

She takes him little by little,

All around him,
Trying to retrieve his hand in vain,
To save him from the beaten paths,
Where illness gains ground,

With impunity, leaving him defeated.

-     The disease

Death took him away,
In the midst of the beautiful season,
A lightning bolt pierced my heart,
Leaving only ashes,
Of sorrow and pain,
Of despair and anger.

I hold a grudge against cancer,
For taking his life on Earth.

I think of him every time,
Memories spring forth,
Here or there,
Fragments deafen,
Every word,
That I try to express,
Every time he wasn't there,
Far from me, yet close to my heart,
In a world where he wasn't far,
Near me, close to my soul.

The sky was grey,
The sun was hidden,
Behind a mountain of clouds,
A thick disturbance,
That covered a bad omen,
Everyone was crying,
Trying to remain composed,
In the face of intense affliction,
From his departure,
The heart sways,
Through sadness and fog.

At dawn, I searched for him,
But he was no longer there,
He had promised to return,
But it's just a memory,
They said they didn't know,
If one day he would leave,
From those white walls,
In which his light was fading,
Another morning where I search for him,
Tears echo in the silence,
The sorrow is immense,
My heart refrains,
From shattering into a thousand pieces,
If only I had the words.

- End

Grief knows no rules,
Each for oneself,
Deciding how to face the hell,
Of a life with a bitter taste,

There is no right process,
The journey of life must continue its
narrative,
With a gaping wound on a fevered heart.

The universe cracks under the moon,
The effect of a world without transfer,
It's the drowning of the gaps,
The fault in the atmosphere.

- Chaos

The past resurfaces incessantly,
Stopping it is not possible.

The wounds still raw from the past only
bleed when thoughts are too strong.

-    The past is a vicious circle.

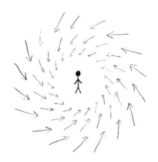

Nothing is familiar anymore, melancholy is indefinable, I was searching for words and then, nothing, again.

Like those days when the sky weeps, and the deluge descends upon me.

My consciousness is numb, I refuse to accept, it's stronger than me, I wish to distract myself, if only for a song, or a lifetime.

- Despair of words

I disregarded each day,
Reliving the pain of the one who broke my
heart,
It was a spring morning,
Yet the beauty of twilight has forever faded
away.

My thoughts burn within me,
They consume me and disarm me,
In this blazing fire,
From which I can't feel the warmth,
Only the pain of my heart dying in the
inferno,
I remain frozen before the charred remains
of our lives,
The smoke that escapes bears witness to
our memories,
And all our unfinished dreams.

-   Grief is a heart set on fire

I dipped my pen into my tears to write these words.

Is there an angel to tell him,
That I have despised every sunrise,
For none of them brought him back,
That I have reversed the norms,
Broken the rules,
That I have tried to still believe,
When resentment and disorder reign in my
heart,
That I am sorry,
Sorry for being myself,
That I did not want all of this,
Grief is not a take-it-or-leave-it matter,
It envelops in its black shroud,
Without even allowing time to breathe,
The spiral suffocates the evening,
Making us victims of each day.

- Message to an angel

As if everything is decaying, the markers around me lie in ruins,
On the horizon, I glimpse the devastation caused by your disappearance.

- Devastated horizon

In the soul of a child, grief is a heavy
shadow,
A burden that haunts,
It's the turmoil and shock that enter into
torment,
Laughter fades, suffering silently inhabits
their little being,
Then emotions overflow from this
immense void,
Chaos takes hold,
The child falls into the abyss,
Of this lingering wound that torments,
The absent kisses they suffer from,
Extinguish the spark within them.

I inherited the anguish of being,
From my grandparents or perhaps even
further,
Pain is engraved within us,
He set himself free, with a bullet to the
head,
On a day when he couldn't see the end,
Refusing to coexist with his suffering,
He chose to become an absence,
Leaving behind,
A pack of cigarettes and a small note.

-       Tragic departure

As time passes, some memories become inaudible.

I regret that he never saw the sea,
The mountains, the cities, and the lands,
That he never had a chance to express his
anger,
I am disgusted that fate was so relentless,
A condemned child before he could even
walk,
I envy the stars for being able to share his
baby laughter.

His disappearance is life coming to a halt,
It's the world collapsing,
The heart retiring,
Weary of seeking meaning in profound
tragedies,
It's the paralysis of words echoing,
Such a small being, who never had a chance
to be,
Indescribable is the loss,
In the hearts of those who remain,
Petrified in time, memories only ripen,
Accompanied by love that nothing can stop.

The absence is a tornado that ejects from the real world, making one feel the blizzard it holds within.

Shameful to admit,
That this grief obsesses me,
It troubles my mind,
Fear of not being able to justify it,
Too real to display,
Within me, it gets lost,
Illegitimate pain that entwines me.

I rejoice in being able to still dream,
To catch a glimpse of you through my
dreams,
To be able to love you somewhere on this
earth, still.

Twilight had carried her away into a buried fantasy deep within her heart. A supposedly unattainable desire, and yet she knew that nothing was impossible as long as we continue to enrich our imagination, as long as we strive to surpass psychological barriers to become filmmakers.

At dawn, the church bell chased away the night for a return to life, without utopia and without magic.

A morning seemingly like any other, where the sounds of the city and the residents of the neighborhood resound. In the background, nature stirs, the wind blows through the windows, now the birds chirp loudly, and a ray of sunlight bursts forth. However, this dawn was not ordinary. In her mind, she couldn't distinguish what belonged to her sad reality and what was merely the product of her subconscious. During the darkness of the night, she had received the most beautiful gift from it, the dream of them being together, reunited beyond time and space.

All emotions formed a unique feeling in her heart, causing an unprecedented sense of well-being in her soul. A disturbing yet reassuring feeling at the same time.

Her soul was comforted during her sleep, like a child whose tears are dried, revealing a radiant smile on their face. Her soul had regained its color, the color of peace. She had managed to put a bandage on her still-open wounds, leaving only her mind autonomous, leading her towards what she needed, feeling his presence vibrating within her. A new air, like an east wind that rejuvenates the heart by giving it a dose of freshness and sweetness. Like after a long-awaited return to one's roots. That was the case. The day before, sitting at the foot of a tree, contemplating the horizon and its wonders, she wondered where he could possibly be in this landscape, and she searched for him, with despair and clumsiness. Since he had left, she spent her time trying to find fragments of him in everything she pursued, in everything she read, in everything she heard.

That's what the void provoked in her, the bitter search for the one to whom she owed her life, the one who taught her everything except how to live without him.

But in her reality, in full consciousness, she gradually lost the memories of that person she considered precious, the sound of his voice, his bursts of laughter, his gaze...
It was in her dreams that she found him and all her memories came back to life.
In a distant dimension, created by her own brain, she entered the heart of her beliefs, between devotion and curiosity. It was a vast space, brightly and clearly lit, bordering on white, where it was neither too hot nor too cold, where the air was pure, and where a soothing melody resonated.
Each being present seemed in total harmony with the surrounding environment.
Beautiful doves twirled and sang in unison.
It was here, in this spectacular and dreamlike place, that the illusion of their reunion began.
Once she had entered this place, which could be described as paradise, the pain subsided, and nothing seemed to touch her anymore.
She felt disconnected from every fragment of pain that perished within her.
She discovered this place, her eyes sparkling, as every fragment of this place was admirable. Her heart raced; she felt it

beating so strongly in her chest. She moved forward without knowing where to go, but she knew perfectly well where she had come from.

Then, as she crossed the light, he arrived, just as majestic as in her memories, but here, he seemed to no longer suffer. As if the pain had flown away, withdrawn from his body, or perhaps it had remained down here, causing sadness and distress for those who stayed since his departure.

He was dressed in beautiful clothes, his hair well-groom, his face expressing joy and gratitude. She hurried towards him, clinging to his neck, never wanting to let go. The man who occupied every thought, whom she hadn't been able to say goodbye to and express her love one last time, was right there, facing her, as if to console her suffering heart, deprived of him.

This moment represented eternity, without beginning or end, just an extraordinary present. An event that reignited the flame that time had carried into darkness.

During this timeless moment, with the one she cherished so much, the one whose return she eagerly awaited every day, it was fitting to make up for all those lost moments. A tenderness that pieced together the thousands of fragments of her broken soul. A period of unreality that seemed more real than a lifetime spent on Earth, sincere, true, and intensely reassuring.

A moment of comfort far more real than a whole lifetime of consciousness. He offered her once again a source of life, a surge of happiness, as if to alleviate the sadness and anger that had permeated her being.

After this intensely rich night, she woke up, reassured, feeling protected and far from anything that would try to harm her. She understood that dreaming can sometimes help confront the despair of a child. Dreaming is experiencing unexpected moments that bring back to life, offering the heart the oxygen it needs. Dreaming is also bringing life to where one seeks glimmers of hope. It is said that a deceased parent exists in a dream to guide and protect the one who dreams, thus becoming their guardian angel.

- A childhood dream narrative

If I don't see you again in this world,
Meet me in the next,
I won't accept for a second time,
That the universe,
Undeniably keeps you away from me.

I envy the sun for being able to see you still,
I envy the moon for illuminating your dark
sky.

-    As if you were somewhere on Earth

The traces of traumas are indelible.

The nights of my childhood,
Were not filled with fairy tales,
I dreaded finding sleep,
Afraid of being captured,
Going to bed terrified me indiscriminately,
I sought enchantment,
But found disillusionment instead,
So small and vulnerable,
Accompanied by all my troubles,
The afflictions made those nights
unbearable,
After a few years,
Sleep paralysis came into play,
I eventually tamed my fear,
Confronting the tormenting evil.

- Sleep paralysis

On many evenings,
He was there,
Right beside me,
Waiting for me to fall asleep,
To claim my soul,
Waiting for me to weaken,
To drag me into the abyss.

I never saw his face,
Only the sinister shadow of evil,
Targeting a child,
A victim of his repetitive attacks,
Who remained composed,
While he, like an animal,
Made everything deafening.

-    The man with the hat

Childhood dreams that, one fine morning, kill you,

Like the sun dying in the darkness of the night.

If the me of today met the me of ten years ago,
The greeting would be strange,
Like when two strangers exchange a timid smile,
No words would come out of our mouths, no exchange,
We would contemplate each other,
Wondering how is it possible that one day,
We were the other.

-      Change

Through this journey I have led,
The journey of early youth,
I fought against the sorrow,

On a path strewn with explosives,
Grief is aggressive,
The journey is abrasive,
Animated by sad twists and turns,
Shattering the delicate heart,

To make room for ebony black sorrow.

Grown in a fraction of a second,
As if to reach the moment,
Where I would feel strength flow through
my veins,
As if the summit was consciousness,
As if time would resolve the turmoil,
I wished to break the chains that protected
me,
To become that wild flower, free and
untamed,
I wanted to grow, I thought it was the key,
But I was swept away by what traumas
create,
When unconsciousness shatters,
When family loses faith,
When there is no law left,

Being sad was my only right.

Thrown out of my childhood,
My innocence ripped away,
Like a common package,
And when awareness came,
My soul was shredded,
I ended up at sea, like waste,
Thrown away by an ignorant,
Who knows no other way to live,
Than by rotting everything around him.

Let's take a stroll,
Discover love,
Cupid and his greed,
Eros and his mistakes.

Let's observe fear,
The tremors of the heart,
And the piled-up dreams.

Let's encounter depression,
Its phases of introspection,
The path of repression,
Life crumbling away,
What demons harbor,
In their malevolent days.

Let's try to see,
What the evening looks like,
When disappointment prevails,
When sorrow reigns,
When the heart stagnates,
Feelings bleeding.

- A poem of a thousand ill

AWARENESS

Some flowers will wither away,
Forever it seems,
Others will resist,
Wage war against the years,
Weeds will grow,
Covering the field of wheat.

Inevitably.

Everything is raw, tenderness was lost on a drunken night,
A leaf, a pen, a bath of sadness.

-    2017

Often neglected,
I tried to catch up with the past,
Thinking I could change it,
It haunted me, shattered me,
I faced the danger,
When the moon shines,
In the depths of the night,
The cold and the darkness,
Create in my heart,
An intense and empty fog,
Without a soulmate.

- Disconnected

Absence is a void,
Making grief too present,
There's nothing left to hold,
The heart sustains itself,
With loneliness and incomprehension,
The only remedy is time,
Which passes without altercation.

The mind wanders,
Through all these waves,
Like a burst of laughter,
Coming to console sadness,
The memories of the worst,
The regrets it leaves behind,
Comes the impact of a bomb,
Even to the graves,
That make the souls shudder,
Suddenly, inevitably,
When the drama suddenly erupts,
The deafening noise,
Of a world collapsing,
Right there, in front of the crowd,
A cluster of pale humans,
Unable to fight against,
The tragic end of the guide.

-    The explosion of the drama

I dream of you when I sleep,
And my heart withers.

Flower grown in the shadows,
Drawn to the darkness.

Fallen angel,
Alone before the distorted mirror.

- During

What could kill you, if not yourself ?
Using your brain as a tool of torture.

-	Enemy

Maybe you are like me,
Maybe many of us are in this situation,
Remaining paralyzed,
Like an oryx in front of a feline,
Allowing oneself to be devoured without
uttering a word,
Too occupied with being killed,

Trapped by yourself,
Aren't you your own predator?

- Victim of oneself

The unconscious seeks refuge
In familiar comfort zones,
Even if they are toxic,
Scattering the forgetfulness
Of a vulnerable heart's purity.

-     Working on the unconscious

To rethink is to dive,
Reopening the wound that withered us,

Obsessed child,
By what once was,
The cause of my insanities.

Life assaults us in the face,
Leaving us with wounds to mend,
Victims of our sutures,
Hoping to see them dissolve someday.

-    Wounds of life

The sky cries to wash away our distortions.

-   Rainy day

I will burn my regrets,
As my faults are shot through my mind,
The heat of pain,
Enchanting the soul in weightlessness,
Love lost on a winter evening,
The heart as cold as the universe,
The sun no longer shines so beautifully,
Tears flow abundantly,
For those promises that ended,
In the heart of nothingness, shattered and
deprived.

Lost in this insane dimension,
My body is but a rental,
A foreign vehicle I drive without direction.

- Unknown body

I don't want to deceive myself,
I prefer to torment my mind.
Living in this persistent darkness,
That makes life less beautiful,
That favors suffering over ignorance,
Keeping me away from disdain in excess.

- Understanding pain

I was sad, wondering why,
I encountered sorrow when I least
expected it,
I faced grief when I didn't want to,
I felt tears flowing when I had no control,
I saw my heart crumbling, unable to heal it,
I witnessed the world collapsing, unable to
change anything,
I experienced love, only to see it scatter.
I observed time passing, childhood tearing
apart, flowers withering, adolescence
tormenting itself, memories dividing, life
rusting away, in complete darkness.

-    The answer to "why"

It leaves lifeless bodies,
Beaten down and devoid of any desire,
The only longing remains to let everything
fly away,
To let go, to unravel it all.

- Depression

I believe that one day life killed me.

Lived in silence,
Unnamed depression,
Shielded by silence,
To the point of believing my own absence,
I sought to nourish it,
Or to no longer suffer,
Describing what I was experiencing,
Seemed unattainable,
Sometimes it was laughable,
Distinguishing madness from illness,
Understanding the dreadful solitude,
The one that made me incapable,
Of getting out of bed,
Of enjoying life,
Of having an appetite,
Sadness was a deadly poison.

-   Bitter sorrow

I will wipe away your tears,
Amidst the shimmering lights,
Reflecting in the depths of your eyes,

In an intense void,
Where heart and soul lack dance,
I will embrace your sorrows,
Facing the sun, at the foot of the plain.

- Sharing sorrows

I intoxicated myself with my wounds,
My mind got entangled in them,
To give meaning to my phases,
Baring myself in a few phrases.

- Exhibition

Having fallen blindly into the trap
Of the whims of unfortunate processions,
If I had succeeded,
I wouldn't have been able to see,
All those vibrant sunrises,
All those comforting sunsets.

-    If

I wanted to escape,
Ready to tear open my chest,
To stop dancing,
To stop thinking,
To stop drowning.

- Elusive substance

I realized that blood was flowing,
Once the tears can no longer,
Allow the wounds to bleed,
It's not an excess of weakness,
Nor a synonym for cowardice,

It is only after that the healing can begin.

Sometimes it rains,
Torrents of anger,
Showers of sadness,
While outside the sky is radiant.

-     Inside your mind

After years of downpours,
Roofs are battered,
Like after a fierce battle,
With drops that cut both ways,
All those tears of rain,
Explode intensely,
Rain is in constant motion,
It goes away and comes back,
Flooding everything without drying,
Each fragment drowning the heart,
All the pearls from the sky that shower the
face.

That's what I call pain,
The eternal cycle,
Of a pounding rain,
When the sun fails to illuminate the storm.

Sleep eludes me,
As insomnia awakens in the evening,
Depressive phases,
Are often too aggressive.

Sometimes I wait for the first rays of the sun,
Hoping they will guide me,
Longing for them to steer me,
But the night has faded away,
And the sandman has passed by.

My nightmares take me,
Sometimes in a different perspective,
In which I feel,
The pain of space,
The sense of being in the wrong place,
No longer able to distinguish truth from
falsehood,
As if everything existed and yet nothing at
all.

- Nightmare reality

Throughout its cycle, the moon goes
through eight phases,
In which it reveals itself over time,
Similar to the mind, during a minute of
insomnia,
Where the murmurs of the brain twist into
a violent breath.

- Insomnia

Sleep disorder, go away,
I no longer want to wait,
For you to decide for me,
In the evening, you devour me,
Like an animal and its prey,
I never doubted you,
You weave all sorts of webs,
Without relying on the stars,
Nocturnal spider,
What will be next ?

I don't know what to do,
When my limbs tremble,
When my heart seems,
To have detached from my arteries,
Vivid impulses and inner screams,
Animate my nights in the cold.

-     Anxiety

The tears of the night,
Spin my mind around,
From these buried feelings,
I feel bored.

- When they come back

Flooding my mind with thoughts,
Sometimes makes me sway,
If it were a choice,
I would distance myself from it,
Before diving back in.

- Choice

The heart melts in the foam of an ocean of thoughts.

Life is not a river of fresh water,
Splashing happiness as if it were raining,
It's an ocean on which you choose to sail,
With the direction of the waves,
Or against the current,
Sometimes you wander off course,
But you can't run away,
You would drown before even trying.

-    Confronting

If happiness knocks on my door one day,
I would ask it to stay,
To take the time to savor,
A coffee during the summer solstice.

-     Visit of happiness

ENTANGLEMENT

Just a lost soul,
Seeking a paternal figure,
Wandering through twisted loves,
Lost in endless quarrels.

The love I gave you,
The energy and time,
Did not deserve to wither,
Ruined by your misguided heart.

Love, desire, illusion,
Relationship, disorder, loss,
Never, one day, always,
There it is, the hurricane...

- Toxic wave

Your lie eats away at me,
My sorrow lingers on,
My body stretches,
Overflowing with dreams,
My heart is a sponge,
Diving into a dream.

You disappear into my eyes,
The water seemed gentle to you,
Didn't you see the troubled waters ?
The icy paths,
Floating on the surface,
Stripped of their origins,
The ground like a minefield,
Crumbling beneath the tide,
But you saw nothing,
Blinded by your thoughts.

Why do I think of you,
When the sun sets,
As if you were
Only a shadow of myself.

You left,
Without a word,
Silence and ignorance,
You seemed to fly,
Above my feelings,
Without even acknowledging them,
Because deep down,
It wasn't your concern,
It was me who suffered,
While you,
Didn't even bruise a wing.

- Ignorance

I think of you,
The nights by your side,
The days without you,
Remembering that your being,
Made me sick,
Reminding myself that my being,
Cannot be healed by you.

-       Love poison

Is there any part of me left in you,
Embedded in your arms,
Is there any trace of faith,
When the day fades behind the sheets,
And the darkness takes its hold.

My heart still loved you,
But my mind no longer wanted to,
Of this hardcore love,
That brought, as a bonus,
The feeling of being dead.

- Dead love

I would like to see you one last time,
Maybe a multitude of last times,
To savor your scent like fresh air in my
windpipe,
To promise you that I will never attach
myself again,
That I will eventually erase you from my
thoughts,
But to feel you close to me, for an hour or a
night,
Just to feel the desire in your sighs,
To annihilate myself in your pleasures.

-    Last time

I can't believe,
That I loved you,
More than I loved myself.

When your sweet words healed my harsh
pains,
I felt blessed,
When your harsh words tore my heart
apart,
I remained in denial.

I acted out of love,
While you played your tricks,
Now,
I no longer want this love,
Existing only at night out of fear of the day,
A partial and unbalanced feeling,
That scars, like an ugly emotion,
You will remember me,
Complete love that doesn't change with the seasons,
You will wonder, which of us was right ?

-    Lingering feeling

And yet, you,
I know you loved me,
Saw in me,
What others couldn't see,
But I,
Didn't know how to act,
Didn't know how to feel,
Like the art of war,
What we desire,
Is never what we feel,
Influenced by customs,
And everything that remains,
In me like residues,
Of my lost love.

-    If I knew how to love you

One day,
I had to leave,
Stop giving myself,
To see you smile,
Stop believing in you,
To see myself suffer,
So I let go,
I was no longer acquired.

- One day I left

It's a shame our promises are forever just dust,
Lost words through time.

Tell me about her dreams,
About all her wild desires,
Tell me what animates her,
All that forms an ocean of thoughts in her
heart, similar to sparkling stars in space,
Tell me what breaks her heart,
The daily events that bring forth a torrent
of tears on her gentle face,
Tell me about her fears during the day that
follow her into her darkest nights,
About what scares her and makes her
nauseous,
Tell me about her inner strength,
About everything she has been through to
get here, the tumultuous trials of life,
Tell me about who she was as a child,
About what made up her little being, filled
with perfect innocence,
Tell me about who she wants to be or what
she's trying to become,
About her daily struggles to exist as she
wishes.

-     Knowledge

After experiencing it in all its forms,
How many lose faith in love?

Disappointment takes hold of me when
I dwell,
On all those moments spent in your arms,
Believing I belonged.

It's an accident of feelings, like a knife being plunged deeply into your back, the torment is profound and brings about twists and turns.
Feelings clash,
Fear, doubt, anguish, bad memories.
When the heart gets involved, it trembles, it weeps.

-     Vulnerable

I no longer want to remember,
So I erase our photos one by one,
Believing I'm resigning to your desertion,
Trying to never remember again,
That one day you left without even turning
back.

- Lost friendship

Inside me echo the sounds of your voice,
Those that shattered me,
Those that tormented me,
Those that I loved so much.

So predictable,
Love is sometimes laughable,
You will eventually have me to yourself,
And you will leave,
The day you want me, I will be there, my
love,
I will wait for you to need me,
I will wait for you to desire me forever,
For my entire being to obsess you,
Then I will leave.

- Toxic

I will never love someone enough to let
them see me in all my states,
Or perhaps I will love them too much to
condemn them to face it with me.

- My sorrow belongs to me

I don't know if I still love you,
Or if I love the illusion of our love.

I loved watching the stars in your arms,
Each sparkle shone brighter when you
were there,
Now when I look at them alone,
They constantly remind me of you,
Glistening,
Yet so distant.

- Stars in the eyes

I accepted seeing you only at night,
To admire your sparkling eyes,
The crescent moon,
As the sole witness to our embrace.

- Dark possession

Can love be killed,
With a fork or a knife,
To no longer feel,
The absence of your smile.

Fire dehumanized me,
Feelings became automated,
Allowing the flame to diminish,
The moments passed,
Perish in the blaze,
I must rebuild my love with a bulldozer.

My heart is under construction, will you
help me rebuild it ?
Or like the others, will you let my love
perish in the concrete ?

I never thought I would forget you,
Like winter forgets,
The flowers of spring,
Even when the light emerges,
For us, it was only a moment,
My heart is healed,
I crossed it out,
The dancing memories,
Of you and me.

-     One day love leaves

You sowed a field of black roses in me.

II TOMORROW AT DAWN

The sun rises, radiant and captivating,
After a restless night.

HEART

Toxic emotions alternate the flavor of love,
Yet love reigns supreme, I am in love with
love, the kind that transcends time.

Love is unfathomable, elusive, and eternal.

If I were to define the supernatural force,
I would not hesitate, it is her
She could witness the world burn without
faltering,
She always finds a reason to move forward.
She would jump in with both feet to help,
But she has never needed help.
She has always found the remedy,
On its shoulders, she has carried
everything,
As if she is endowed with divinity.
She is the essence of my existence,
The heroine who gave me life.

- Mother

She worked so hard,
Just look at her hands full of scars,
Little cuts, damaged nails,
She never let time persecute her,
She fought every day,
To offer her children
A life filled with love.

-     Resilience

Among the most beautiful moments of my life,
Are those moments when mom recalls her youth,
Her memories and smiles,
Fill my heart with tenderness,
Nostalgia is imprinted in hers,
But immense is her gratitude for those adventures,
For that beautiful journey.

- Time of before

The years of my childhood,
Roaming through pavilions and alleys,
Between friends and quarrels,
Sitting in a park, gazing at the sky,
Being able to talk and laugh for hours,
Nothing could stop us,
Not even the passing time,
Far from technology,
From all external distractions,
We enjoyed the sun and admired every
flower,
The light of the day unfolded before our
eyes,
The fragrance of those moments was
fabulous.

- Nostalgia

Responsible for my first breath,
Her courage seizes me,
When my world is suffocating.

The security of deep love,
The one that grows every day,
To climb the towers,
Unbreakable and indelible,
A precious golden thread,
To cherish like a treasure.

- The one who gives life

The strength of bonds,
Breaks the chains of my sorrows,
The complicity of my loved ones,
Beautifies my words.

-     Bonds of love

The time for tears,
Replaced by the laughter of my sisters,
Who illuminate every flower,
Growing in my heart.

Life can never extinguish,
The hearts of those who love passionately,
Devotion and loyalty,
The one that burns with a thousand fires,
With their amorous feelings.

I see them dancing,
Laughing and colliding,
Taking pleasure,
Through their desires,
When I watch them,
I feel deep within me,
That the world is at my feet,
That they are the essence,
That allows me to move forward.

Somewhere on Earth,
There will always be someone to love,
A being to ignite,
Everything that shines,
A heart to affect,
A part of mine.

- Love never dies

It is pointless,
To traverse infinite lands,
Accompanied by a thousand souls crazed
with madness,
Surround yourself with those who are
unlike any other on Earth,
Invest in them your love,
The kind that doesn't waver when the rain
falls,
Give them everything you have to offer,
Without reservation, without pretense,
Through day and night.

- Surroundings

I have chosen certain angels,
To build a family,
With invisible bonds,
That nothing can change,
Beings nourishing my universe,
With a million smiles,
Creating together mountains of memories,
Melodies that will remain,
Words that will be engraved.

-    Friends

The lights twinkle,
Only because you exist,
Don't lose yourself in darkness,
Your eyes sparkle,
Don't let them close,
Because of the night.

I have wandered along the coasts,
suffocating in an ocean of pain, and on one
of those beaches, I found you.
Like a gentle ray of sunshine, you pierced
through my heart, reviving its fragments
and loosening the knot that had formed.
Like a break in the clouds on my path,
You entered the clearing of my soul like a
glimmer of light, understanding my
sorrows, appreciating my flaws.
In the sea of suffocation where I struggled,
the surface seemed unreachable.
But you were there, as if to lift me up, to
show me that there was still air on the
horizon, that not everything was bleak and
unstable.
I feel at peace in your arms, in the arms of
my new life, a better life where pain and
sorrow have been set aside, surpassed by a
happiness that fills the heart, the certainty
of love.

-    A savior's sentiment

On the boulevard of stars, our paths will cross,
We will dance near the moon,
Breathing life into our emotions between Jupiter and Mars,
Sending our hearts twirling on Saturn's ring,
Let us never distance our souls like Pluto and the sun,
Draw closer to Mercury to find warmth,
Without being caught in the icy winds of Uranus,
Let's create a love greater than Neptune.

- Solar system of love

Love, the infinite cosmos,
Where our beings are united,
Wandering stars in the darkness,
Finding their place in the journey of
eternity.

It is their voice that I hear,
A sweet melody,
In my mind, waiting,
For me to rise,
Face what weakens me,
And conquer,
Every challenge.

- The guiding voice

I have locked away in a chest,
Sentenced for eternity,
Countless memories,
Smiles as if they rained down,
Secured with all their fabric.

-    Lock on memories

Writing is to me,
What a bandage is to a wound,
Poetry soothes the pains,
And all the blasphemies.

- Art is a form of love

I have come to love life,
Even adore it,
Like a child,
Enthralled by everything it offers,
I have discovered this new self,
Undeniably in love,
With every detail,
With memories of yore,
With the sea and the wind,
With rain and sunny weather.

I will not let my being,
Take the shape of your despair,
I have made room for celebration,
In hopes of witnessing the true me grow,
Not the one that resided in your heart,
But the one who is wholly itself.

She needed someone to save her,
So she became that person.

Inner well-being,
It's the soul's wave,
Granting a taste of honey with every
awakening,
Enveloped in poetic melodies,
When I lose myself in their embrace.

- Embraced in the arms of my new life

I will continue to nurture,
Every fiber of my being,
With the most beautiful flowers,
Teaching them love,
How to live it,
How to overcome,
The sweetness of inner peace,
Compassion leading to fulfillment,
The pride of petals and thorns.

   -    Self-love is an eternal journey

The paradise may catch fire,
If we are together,
We will build our own sanctuary.

-    Sheltered

Loving you makes me feel alive,
I sense passion within me,
Exploring every path of my mind.

I want us to embrace until the dawn of the end of the world.

-   Forever

I have entrusted you with my intimacy,
In search of shared eternity.

Our hearts entangle,
And our bodies intertwine.

- Desire

Become my muse,
Let our days be intoxicating,
So that together we have fun,
Scream with joy,
Share our desires,
Until the break of dawn.

Today, I miss you,
Tomorrow, I find myself.

Think of the person who hurt you the most,
Feel the pain they inflicted upon you,
Recall the tears that were shed,
Visualize your most beautiful memories,
Now, let them die,
Like your sorrow,
That holds you back,
Let it flee.

- Let memories fly away

Embrace the love of others,
Accept each compliment,
And try to believe in them a little,
Let them cover your heart,
They love you for who you are entirely,
Feel the peace, they are wonderful.

    -    Others love you

Never forget who you are,
At the expense of what others want you to
be for them,
Create a philosophy,
In line with your desires,
Follow your own path,
The path of self-confidence.

- Just you

Don't be too hard on yourself,
You will make mistakes,
Choose the wrong people,
But at least you had the hope,
That they could have been better,
The people and the choices,
That you pointed your finger at,
In the end, isn't hope for a better future
more beautiful than regret forever ?

-    Keep what's beautiful

You will meet people who will use your heart as an arena in which they want to play the role of the strongest, ready to do anything to come out victorious.

They will try to take control of all the cards, unfairly.

You know what you have that is most precious, this arena, which is yours. Only the players with the hearts cards will remain, those who play loyalty, who love you and bring you daily well-being.

You are the only one with power over this arena. Show the exit to the bad players and take care of those who deserve their place. Keep this arena as a place of peace and happiness.

- The arena of the heart

HEALING

Acceptance was the most beautiful flower,
No need for a doctor,
Nor the kiss of an ocean of liquor,
Just purify my heart,
From my own resentments,
I gave myself the right,
To be sad and to be myself,
To be afraid and to feel cold,
To offer my mistakes,
To not let fear lead,
To try to become better,
To free my inner self,
To feel the warmth of the world,
I did myself a favor.

After the storm,
Sweetness returned,
Losses,
Crash,
Traumas,
Pieces of myself,
Scattered along the path,
Like eraser dust,
Despair is a ghost,
I built my consciousness on its footprints.

When the cause departed,
I tracked down the foundations of reasons,

When I'm feeling down,
Believing even in the evening,
That bitterness will fade away,
That I will be freed from myself,

Healing was the home,
Waiting for me to take a pause.

-       Embracing

When clarity rises,
And darkness is seen dying,
When my heart goes on strike,
Writing makes me come alive,
One day, writing saved me,
For days, I hadn't seen the rising sun,
Only a dying sun,

Writing,
Setting sun,
Night,
Rising sun.

This past year,
Was shaped,
Like a chain of mountains,
That I decided to climb,
One after another.

Time, a puzzle of surprises,
I thought I know myself for a long time,
But I have learned more about myself,
In few months of total existence,
Than in years of coexisting with myself.

- When I was running away from
  being myself

I wanted to tell you that I missed you,
I tried to catch a glimpse of you,
But the light was distant,
I tried to get closer,
But it was impossible to see,
Through the mountains,
While you were there,
Hidden deep inside me,
Deprived of your freedom to shine.

-    The sun within me

Your presence in my life,
Simply reminded me,
That before being *us*,
I had to be myself.

Born on the first day of the week,
To see nothing escape,
A ray of sunshine in the middle of summer
Growing up in a wintry world.

\-   A summer monday

And then I fell,
I had never experienced such a beautiful
fall,
Although the rock scratches,
The landing made me new.

- My mountain

Let the sky,
Turn our quarrels,
Into poems for everyday,
Into sparks forever.

If flowers no longer want to grow,
Don't try to save them,
Understand them in their entirety,
They need to wither,
Rot and regenerate,
Sometimes, even the strongest flowers are
exhausted.

- Letting go

Throwing stones into the sea,
Out of despair or therapy,
Screaming to see nothing anymore,
That day the sky was gray,
But our minds were free,
Trying to maintain balance,
Broken pieces,
Of a glass bottle.

-     Sadness by the sea

I refuse to harm my life,
I love each passing day,
Even if the pain surpasses,
Sometimes the awakening sun,
I escape from my bed,
To run after awakening.

I composed all my wealth by loving this world,
By feeling gratitude for every second.

Your comfort zone,
Is nothing but a prison,
Where you decide,
To lock up your body,
You create your home there,
No by choice, but disappointment,
Without leaving room for signs,
You slide in the troubles,
Of your irresistible subconscious,
Which makes it invisible,
This prison where you stay,
Out of fear of change,
Of leaving your past life,
Fear of happiness.

- Departing

If you believe that happiness,
Is found elsewhere,
Escape,
Without taking your fears with you,
Travel with a light heart,
Free and weightless,
Just a suitcase full of flowers,
And your reason to guide you.

-     Suitcase of the heart

I will not fill my heart with hatred,
Nor with sorrow,
For all those who crossed my path,
And wanted to throw me to the lions
It was surely my destiny,
To understand that they were the lions.

- World of ferocity

To be at peace with oneself,
Is to be at peace with the world,
To satisfy oneself,
To please oneself,
To let go,
Of harmful codes,
To create a vast,
Inner world,
That makes space vibrate.

They always say we have time to live, time to love, discover, see, or feel.
If we stopped wasting this time telling ourselves that it will surely happen in the near future.
And if we started dreaming.
And if we did everything to provoke what animates us.

I want to return to the sea,
Like a child to its mother,
To disappear across the horizon,
Watching the seasons pass.

To this day,
I could still suffer to death,
I could spend my nights crying,
But I have decided to live differently,
Not to let the fate of life,
Make me suffer the worst punishment,
The one of not believing in happiness,
And of living only through unhappiness,
Not to let others,
Damage me for useless purposes.

-     In ten years, what will you
      remember ?

When I feel tested,
I set myself a challenge,
To revive my vibration,
At the height of my imagination,
Not to let myself be lulled,
By pain for too long,

And I rise from my ashes,
Like a triumphant phoenix.

When life hurts me,
I write, to the point of losing sight,
I write, I expose myself,
I write,
Without understanding the meaning of
words,
Or the meaning of my sorrows,
I write,
Until the day breaks,
And my mind makes peace.

-    Finding an escape

Monday, August 8, 2022,

During my vacation in the South, I went hiking in the cliffs, between two small coastal towns, alone. Arriving at the end point, I sat on a terrace, a glass in hand, filled with an ocean of varied thoughts. In my ears, sweet melodies of Sofiane Pamart, Tom Rosenthal, Fabrizio Paterlini, Claude Debussy flowed, accompanying the journey of my feelings.

With my eyes turned towards life, towards all those people who were enjoying their days away from routine, with eyes full of happiness, the sea shimmered on the horizon, the sun cherished their hearts, children laughed, and birds danced above this moment of eternity. This plunged me into deep reflection.

I embarked on a little introspection, allowing my pen to write it down.

Note to myself to never forget :

From my earliest childhood to now, the awakening of my twenties, from my first phases to the most recent ones. Enough to realize a multitude of words.

And you should, at least once, take a moment in your life and recap it, just to realize that your Story has a much simpler summary than you imagine, and so that in the future, you stop slowing yourself down until you stop for events that will have no importance in ten years. Throughout our existence, we face adventures, we go through moods, torrents of tears, and bursts of joy.

We meet people whom we would have wanted to love for our entire lives, yet they leave when the time comes, at the end of our shared adventure.

By taking stock of our entire History, it is the essence that escapes, and this fundamental essence includes few facts compared to everything we have experienced in its entirety.

I have noticed that we spend a phenomenal amount of time dwelling on certain moments, certain people, who, in the end, represent only a tiny fraction of our greater selves, in the History of our journey. If I speak of History, with a capital H, it's because it deserves that capital. In the name of our struggles, our values, our education first elaborated by the conditioning in which we evolved, and the one we have crafted ourselves. Our own learning of life, our way of loving it or hating it, our worldview that makes each of us undeniably unique beings.

It encompasses the events that have made you the adult you are, the tumultuous trials that have made you feel alive or on the verge of dying, those beings who have made your life a dream or a nightmare and have marked it for better or worse. Taking stock of the essence is realizing that, at any given moment, we can spend hours losing ourselves in a problem, a constraint, regardless of its gravity, in relationships, be they friendships, romantic, or professional.

We can spend sleepless nights out of apprehension for an important upcoming situation, out of sadness due to a conflict with a loved one, crying, screaming, or simply feeling depressed, and this concerns a great deal of facts, whatever they may be. And even worse, however insignificant they may be.

Precisely, all these facts, all the reasons for our moments of doubt, weakness, we don't really remember them a few years later; we forget the "why."

Why we cried, why we fueled relentless hatred, why we lamented for so long, why we subjected our own brain to endless questioning, torturing our minds over trivial matters. These vanities ultimately do not belong to the recapitulation of your life; they have not marked it; they have simply animated your daily life during a particular period. Of course, all these small details without real importance now may have helped you learn, grow, perceive elements in a different way at the time they were experienced.

Now, they are only scattered fragments of dust wandering through time and are not key points in your History. Remember that

the only moment you possess is the present,
and it is you who decides your reality. Yet, at
the moment it happens, everything seems to
unfold as the end of the world. A few years
later, we will only remember that there are
great moments in life that we will never
erase. Always people whom we will
remember because they mattered to us,
because they were there at a moment in life
when we needed them, because they left
their mark on our lives in their own way.
Important moments, enormous sorrows, and
indescribable joys. It is wise not to pollute
our memories with what does not belong.
Memory is an infinite treasure, knowing
what truly belongs to it is priceless.

-     Excerpt of my diary

One day he uttered a sentence that resides deep within my soul, between heart and consciousness. Ever since, it animates me, and I feel it is the essence of a growing power within me, an inexplicable force that makes me believe and hope at the same time, like a sign from beyond.
I could cross the seas, even if it means drowning. Scale the mountains, even if it means falling into the abyss of failure. Wander through endless fields, even if it means getting lost.

For my dreams, I would do it, without losing hope, endeavoring to become the best version of myself. The passing of time reminds me of who I am, where I come from, and why I am here.
Why I breathe, why I write, why I cry.

It has given me strength, good faith, a beautiful and rebellious soul when words and afflictions that bring my spirit down depart.
Moments pass faster than music, the speed of light doesn't scare me much, because faster than it, I will sprint towards merit.

Life teaches us that the best is yet to come, only if we wait for it. That the future can knock on the door in a transcendental manner, provided we wish to let it in.

That deposits from a time when we believed in them more strongly than now reside nearby.

- *The sentence that dad spoke, engraved in time*

Living above the norms,
Breaking the codes,
Becoming oneself,
Becoming a king.

-    King tomorrow

You have the choice,
You can remain seated,
Contemplating the cold,
You can defy the laws,
Discovering life from the highest roof.

- All you have to do is believe

Let the inner flame burn,
Nourish it with your grandest dreams,
With your overflowing hopes,
Let it set ablaze your fears and invasive
memories,
Be the sun that illuminates your destiny,
Without letting doubt sow darkness.

Raise your vibration,
Expand your beliefs,
Let the notions grow,
That create kindness,
Don't be afraid to believe,
If you find yourself,
If you become whole,
You are free,
But respect,
The one who believes,
The one who doesn't believe,
The one who doubts,
The one who seeks his path,
The journey and its destiny,
Deserve to be preserved.

-    Free to be

Rise and continue to believe,
In the victory of light,
Facing the shadows that surround you,
Draw inspiration from your pain,
To repaint your sky,
In the colors of the sun.

- Painting with an open heart

Think, reflect, coordinate your ideas.
But don't forget to breathe.

- Knowing how to exist

Don't let anyone tell you it's your fault,
They could never understand,
That the brain is programmed to freeze,
When a situation is too difficult,
To never become docile,
They won't be able to imagine,
The ice that has taken hold of your mind,
Leaving your body almost lifeless,
As if to protect you.

-     Self-protection

Go back to the source of your wounds,
Search for memories and scars,
Swallow them until the last one,
The source is a root,
Buried deep underground,
That you will have to extract,
When you want to heal your wounds.

-    Healing

I don't want to fly away with regrets in my
heart,
I want to be able to savor without worrying
about the taste of tomorrow,
Life tests us with a multitude of obstacles,
Evaluating our abilities and weaknesses,
The truth being that we are capable of the
incredible,
To let the weight of our mistakes and
sorrows sink to the bottom of a well,
Without ever drowning alongside them,
They will never be good company.

Tell him that I escaped from myself,
That it was both the hardest and the most
beautiful battle.

Is there an angel to tell him,
That from now on, I appreciate every
sunrise,
Because they marvel me,
I have started to live again,
Breathe with ease,
Enjoy being intoxicated,
With my benevolence.

The soul studded with fractures,
With shards of light in the darkness,

They are not weaknesses, they are the
forces that guide when everything is dark.

- They define who you are

If the moon crumbles,
Tell her it will be okay,
Tell her she is somewhere,
Healing,
And that time shelters,
For her and her thoughts,
In an art gallery,
A bandage for all her wounds.

Until then, I didn't know,
That magic is magnificent,
When the sun illuminates my words,
And its warmth heals my pains.

I preferred to control the landing instead of witnessing the fall.

- Process

There are moments in existence when you find yourself in an ocean of torments.
The waves echo, the lighthouses alert, but you are already caught in the storm.
You try with all your might to continue your path despite the jolts, but the wind takes you off course and you get lost in the foam.
The ocean is the mind.
And the heart drowns in the mind.
You no longer see the lights of the sky when your feelings are too dark, and when the inner cyclone rages, you no longer distinguish reality.
It's as if you sank with your ship without realizing it.
One day, calm returns, you will find some landmarks.
You will build a makeshift boat with the help of your will to survive. And you will embark, with courage and gratitude.

- A drawing, an inspiration, a story, an artist in Brick Lane

Pushed between shadow and light,
Watered by tears,
In search of a new land,
Shaken by dramas,
Crushed by fear,
She fought for her spark,
Now the sun shines upon her,
And her color becomes idyllic.

-     Blue black rose

Life and death,
The sun and the moon,
The sun, symbol of life, is the fiery ball that gives birth to the day, reveals the truth, and comforts the heart. After its day, it peacefully departs to make way for the moon.
The moon, the mysterious one, lives passively in the darkness, she harbors secrets, and is full of dreams. She is sometimes the only light when darkness takes hold of the sky, she illuminates souls and gives hope when it is not melancholy emanating from her.
Life is death.
The sun is the moon.
One day, the sun and the moon fell in love, but their almost impossible love seemed to have no solution, destined to fail.
They survived, nourishing themselves with each eclipse to become one.

Take the time to admire,
The beauty of spring,
When the wind departs,
The smiles of passersby,
That nothing can erase,
Not even time,
That flows gracefully,
The summer solstices,
In the heart of tides,
The clarity of mountains,
When the mist recedes,
The morning dew,
Covering the grief,
Finally, take the time to breathe.

Today the sun rose at dawn,
Illuminating the sky with its warm rays,
The birds sang for hours,
In the backyard, the most beautiful flowers,
Managed to bloom in the shadow,
The human heart is a resilient shard, it
withers, then blossoms anew, it thrives,
throughout the seasons.

I leave you with these words,
Contemplate my heart in the showcase,
I'm no longer afraid to speak aloud,
Existence is, in my opinion,
A composition full of rhymes,
In which thought expresses itself.

I always thought,
That living made me want to write
thousands of poems.

Poetry,
It's the heart exploding into prose.

Printed in Great Britain
by Amazon

24804107R00119